THE LUST AS A CURSE

PRABH JOT SINGH

Made with ♥ on the Notion Press Platform
www.notionpress.com

Contents

Contents

Preface

The idea for Lust as a Curse was quietly birthed by a nagging question, a thought that sat on my mind: "Why is lust, such a natural human experience, often considered a burden, a fault, or spiritual curse?" I first began pondering this during a conversation with a dear friend, wherein we struggled with the very paradox of lust's power—its ability to unite and to break apart, to kindle desire, and to instill immense suffering.

My journeys took me deep into study: ancient texts, modern psychology, religious instruction, and cultural lore. With that vast span of disciplines, I had come to realize that lust was far more than just a simple drive. It is an immensely multidimensional force that speaks volumes about who we are—our desires, our weaknesses, and the societal frameworks in which we function. The complexity of this issue fascinated me: how lust, at one time, could be seen as a blessed phenomenon and, at another time, could be considered sin; how lust would inspire art, yet would destroy lives and bring sorrow.

With time, and once the questioning deepened, the curiosity matured into an active study. This project has flourished through many hours of researching, reflecting, and dialoging with various scholars, spiritual leaders, and common folk, who have wrestled with them in one way or another. I wanted to really get past the clichés and moral judgments and present a fuller, more complete picture that both honors lust in its raw form and acknowledges its capacity to become a curse when left unmanaged.

The final metamorphosis in the Lust as a Curse is the complete embodiment of this voyage. It serves both as an invitation and a challenge: to face the reality of lust-to understand its power, and how lust may be transformed from an ensnaring force into an enlightening one. I would like the reader to enjoy both a new vantage point and a road to healing.

1

The Understanding of Curse

Curse is a basic tenet in many religious and moral philosophies. It is usually defined to mean an act committed or omitted in contravention of divine law, ethical principles, or societal laws. Curses typically don't involve direct physical action. People believe something invisible (like fate, spirits, or energy) carries it out. If someone says, "May your crops wither and your house fall,"—that's a curse. Of the numerous sins described and debated by philosophers, theologians, and sociologists, lust appears as a special case because of its intricate nature and huge impact on individuals and societies. It is essentially a rupture in nature's equilibrium, for whenever the act of doing, saying, or transmitting energies passes out of congruency with the flux of well-being, disharmony takes precedence a step ahead in that plane of reality. It is less a mystical punishment and more a symbolic reflection of…a curse might almost be considered a representation of consequences—whether actual and external or merely symbolic and internal—that interlude to the break of harmony, trust, and growth. A curse may chain the spirit not through magical means but through repetitive patterns of pain, fear, and unresolved wounds that effectively bind one's potential.

"A curse is not mere magic or fate, but the silent weight of disharmony—an echo of broken balance that binds the spirit through unseen patterns of pain, calling us toward healing and the restoration of inner harmony."

2

The Historical Perspective of Lust

The perception regarding lust spans from ancient texts down to modern interpretations. Lust was never considered shameful in Ancient Mesopotamia and Greece-it was sacred. Ishtar-the goddess of love and war-was the personification of lust and passion. Aphrodite and Venus were not merely beautified icons but irresistible feminine desires that conquered, whether gods or men. Mostly in old religious scripts, lust was condemned for being a powerful and a destructive force. Ancient philosophers and theologians have labeled it as being a base and uncontrolled desire which can lead to moral degradation and socio-economic chaos. In Christianity, especially post-4th century, lust became one of the Seven Deadly Sins. It was linked to temptation, downfall, and spiritual corruption. With the ebb and flow of civilization so has the understanding and representation of lust changed in tune with changing attitudes towards sexuality, morality, and human behavior. It's a force that has built myths, toppled empires, inspired genius, and sparked controversy.

"Lust wears many masks—goddess, demon, muse, and algorithm—reflecting not just desire itself, but the shifting values of each age and the eternal human struggle to define what passion truly means."

3

Lust in Religious Texts

Lust is discussed in numerous religious texts that have varying opinions regarding it and its consequences. In Christianity, lust is rated as one of the seven deadly sins. The Bible stands for purity and self-control by condemning the thoughts of lust or performing the acts. In Islam, lust is just a desire that averts righteousness, hence not encouraged. Hinduism and Buddhism also deal with lust, relating it mostly to desire, which, coupled with other passions, leads a person through the cycle of suffering, binding him to the material world. Adhering to the lines of many religions, the message is clear: lust becomes dangerous not in being, but when it controls human beings instead of being controlled. Gods and Rishis lusted after women. They were aroused by seeing young girls even in their old stricken age. How can I forget to mention Indra in this list after all he frequently lusted after others' wives, I am not saying this but a Sage himself had said it. It is less about denying it and more about constructing discipline around it and balancing it with a certain awareness.

"Lust is not the enemy; it is the flame. When guided, it is sacred; when untamed, it is destructive. Scriptures do not blunt desire; they shape it. They urge the soul to master desire and not to flee from it."

4

Various Theological Interpretations

❧

Prominent theologians have written concerning the dangers of lust, in most cases warning that it is powerful enough to corrupt the human soul and lead one away from spiritual fulfillment. For instance, St. Augustine refers to lust as turning away from God's love to worldly carnal pleasure that looks not to the eternal but to the temporal. Other religious scholars have written on the call to moderation and self-control to move people from their lustful nature. Thus, lust is seen not only as immoral but as a spiritual defect, a curse that causes the body to rebel against the mind. In some Gnostic and mystical traditions, lust is sometimes viewed as indicating that the soul is trapped in a lower, material realm-types and ensounded from being able to awaken. In these theologies, lust is not merely a feeling; it is a spiritual ailment, a sign of internal imbalance, a curse whispering, not just through the body, but also through the fissures that mark the deeper soul's longing for wholeness.

"Lust is more than desire—it is the soul's shadow, a restless echo of imbalance that pulls the spirit away from eternal wholeness into the fleeting prison of the material."

5

The Nature of Lust

Lust can be psychically defined as a very powerfully overwhelming desire for sexual gratification. It is quite an entirely normal feeling in human beings, with biological and hormonal origins. However, if not kept at bay, then it can become obsessive and thus injurious to mental health and well-being. Also lust, in many theological views, is more than desire—it is a spiritual wound, a curse that clouds reason, distorts love, and binds the soul to lower cravings. Seen as a legacy of the Fall, a test of the ego, or a chain of illusion, lust becomes the inner storm that pulls us away from divine clarity and toward restless hunger. Unlike love, which opens and deepens, lust compresses and consumes, narrowing the world into a single object of desire. It is primal yet intelligent, instinctual yet often shaped by culture, fantasy, and memory. Lust is neither good nor evil by nature—it is raw energy, a fire that can warm or burn, depending on whether it's held with awareness or allowed to run wild. It whispers that something outside you will finally fill what's aching inside—but when unexamined, it only deepens the emptiness it promises to cure.

"Lust is raw human energy—neither virtuous nor vile in itself—but a force that tests the soul's clarity; when held with conscious wisdom, it becomes a spark of life, yet when left unchecked, it binds the spirit to illusion and emptiness."

6

The Seed of Desire

—♡—

Lust rarely makes a sudden entry into a life like a thief in the night. Lust grows slowly and quietly- it is often mistaken for something harmless or beautiful. At first, there is nothing but a glance. There is a pull. A warmth that rises inside one at the sight of a person or the imagination of something. One never thinks much about it. Just a thought. Right? A feeling. So, where does lust begin? Does it start in the body? Does it start in the brain? Does lust start in the spirit? Or does it start when we are young and not quite able to understand it, so we begin to pursue it? It might grow in silence—when affection is withheld as we yearn for touch, ultimately for closeness, for intimacy. Not all lust is inherently sexual. Some of it is an "Aye, see me; want me; hold me." Lust for many becomes the first kind of power that people learn: a tool to become noticed, a way to feel important. And then at times, it works. But just like any power, it begins to demand its due. Then, before you even see it, it shoots some roots. It used to just whisper. Now it talks louder than love, louder than reason.

"What starts as a whisper in flesh and bone,
Becomes a hunger when left alone."

7

The Impact of Lust on the Mind

Lust has various psychological effects that pertain to addiction, anxiety, and depression. It makes a change in one's perception of relationships and closeness, objectifying everything and having unrealistic expectations. Knowing the psychological underpinnings of lust is a crucial step toward developing healthier coping mechanisms to increase emotional resilience. Lust enters the mind like a spark in dry grass- sudden, vivid, and consuming. It limits the sight, pushing the attention into a tunnel where urgency weighs heavily upon logic, patience, and long-term consideration. The mind, thus, once expansive and balanced, becomes a fantasy-scape that replays imagined situations with obsessively vivid details. It wastes clarity, for lust quickly replaces reason with impulsive decisions cloaked in passion. At times, lust feeds on love and distorts memories or lures one into believing that satisfaction is merely one fingertip away, intangible hope that, perhaps because it is concealed far too well, only leaves the mind restless and shattered once the actualization settles in.

"Lust ignites the mind like wildfire—vivid, consuming, and blinding—distorting love into obsession and trading lasting meaning for fleeting, restless pleasure."

8

Lust and Social Norms

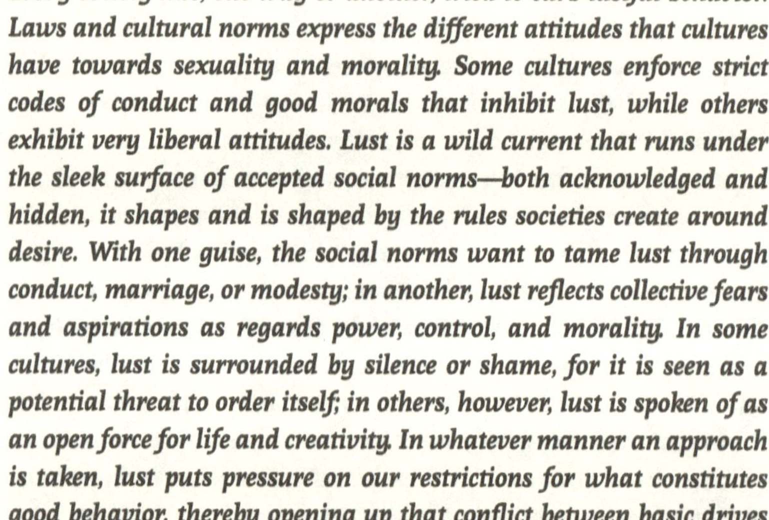

Every society has, one way or another, tried to curb lustful behavior. Laws and cultural norms express the different attitudes that cultures have towards sexuality and morality. Some cultures enforce strict codes of conduct and good morals that inhibit lust, while others exhibit very liberal attitudes. Lust is a wild current that runs under the sleek surface of accepted social norms—both acknowledged and hidden, it shapes and is shaped by the rules societies create around desire. With one guise, the social norms want to tame lust through conduct, marriage, or modesty; in another, lust reflects collective fears and aspirations as regards power, control, and morality. In some cultures, lust is surrounded by silence or shame, for it is seen as a potential threat to order itself; in others, however, lust is spoken of as an open force for life and creativity. In whatever manner an approach is taken, lust puts pressure on our restrictions for what constitutes good behavior, thereby opening up that conflict between basic drives and social values. Between freedom and obligation, lust thus dares challenge societies to find a measure of harmony between the lone individual's passion and public spirit.

"Lust flows beneath society's surface—both tamed by rules and wild
in its rebellion—challenging cultures to balance individual passion
with collective order, forever testing the fragile harmony between
freedom and restraint."

9

The Consequences of Lustful Behavior

The impact of lustful behavior in society may be huge. Some of the results might include family breakups, exploitation of different people, and dangerous practices like human trafficking and pornography. These call for interventions through education, legal reform, and community reinforcement. Dissolving boundaries between feeling and acting, lustful behavior plants within the agent of lust a seed that becomes tangled vines that at first promise a thorn thrills and a sense of connection, later to become adverse clutches around trust, clarity, and peace. The powerful forces of lust parroting one another impair boundaries; acts born of fleeting desire fracture relationships and build up regrets. One by one, the ripples of lustful consequences quietly soar in mind and heart, stirring up distraction, guilt, or emptiness when the burn fades away. They can wreck self-esteem by reducing humans to objects rather than partners, thus setting the stage for systems of craving that prevent the satisfaction of deeper needs. If the spark of lust awakens life, then without restraint, it burns the root of those who cultivate long-term intimacy and real knowing, teaching us that desire coupled with disregard becomes a trap rather than a gift.

"Lust may spark life's fire, but unchecked, it can choke the roots of trust and intimacy—turning fleeting desire into tangled vines that bind hearts with regret and erode the soil of true connection."

10

Defining Morality of Lust

———❦———

Morality is a complex and mostly subjective concept, molded by cultural, religious, and personal beliefs. Defining what constitutes moral behavior concerning lust would require an explanation of values and principles underpinning the various ethical frameworks. Lust itself is morally neutral. It is how we identify, respect, and express that lust that can give it moral status. Lust gains virtue only when it acknowledges the humanity of both the other and self, thereby converting an unmediated urge into a socially relevant experience mutually grounded in consent, honesty, and care. If "Lust" were viewed as an act, then it would be a fleetingly transient impulse in the charge of ephemeral lust based solely on its; otherwise, when acts of lust are considered human acts, they are deliberated willingly and responsively by human beings' conscious choice, balancing with responsibility and respect. Immorally lusting is about denying all conscientious boundaries toward becoming the objectification of the other, thereby disrupting any opportunity for connection or dignity. So, lust`s morality is the dance of honoring respect with desire, with true integrity not manifested in denial but in acceptance and conscious acknowledgment of a person's deepest longings.

"Lust itself is neither good nor bad; its morality unfolds in the dance between desire and respect—where conscious choice transforms impulse into integrity, and longing honors the humanity in both self and other."

11

Lust in the Modern World

———◦♡◦———

Lust does not feel the need to cover up today. It flashes on our screen time, in our music, in an app, scrolls, and swipes. If lust was a temptation before, now it is a full industry. Intimacy does not require knowing someone today. All one needs is a signal and a profile. Conferring, it looks ornery—freedom sans strings. Yet over time, something starts brewing. The sacred can get casual. The emotional turns transactional. And people turn into pixels, into profiles, into placeholders. We've never felt lonelier in this highly connected world. Mistaking sexual access for intimate bonding, cheerleading validation as love. So entertained by the hyper-sexualized lust, it's packaged, sold, and celebrated. But the ramifications are softly stricken. Numbness. Disconnection. The attributed slow damage to wonder and longing. When everything is within reach, nothing feels special. Lust generates sound. The world today is just too loud.

"*In a world that swipes to feel alive,*
We lose the touch for which we strive."

12

Ethical Perspectives on Lust

Different moral theories regard lust from different perspectives. For example, utilitarianism looks at the actions with respect to their consequences, while deontological ethics regards respect and obedience that is owed to rules. Virtue ethics is concerned with the character of a person, his purposes, and motives, seeking the mean between excess and deficiency. In this case, moderation and self-restraint already signify a form of virtue. Ethical considerations concerning lust navigate the rough terrain between what constitutes a natural human desire and the responsibility we bear toward ourselves and others. Some traditions see lust as a natural force that, if appropriately tempered by wisdom and respect, may nurture human bonding and intimacy. Others warn that lust out of control may turn people into mere objects, thereby inciting selfishness and suffering. Thus, in the present context, ethics will assist us in harnessing this great energy of lust without undermining consent, empathy, or integrity. It challenges us to ask not just what we desire but how we pursue it—a place where passion, by mutual consent, balances compassion, where desire itself is not an end but a pathway toward mutual understanding and respect.

"Ethics guides lust from raw impulse to conscious choice—where desire is balanced by respect, passion is tempered with compassion, and the pursuit of pleasure becomes a pathway to mutual understanding."

13

The Illusion of Control

Everyone thinks they can handle it. It's just a little fantasy. Just an innocent message in the wee small hours. Just a little fun and flirting. There are voices inside: You are not addicted. You are just curious. You are in control. But lust is patient. It need not conquer you in one night; just open the door and it awaits. Once inside, it will never leave. Control becomes a facade. You swear to yourself that the next day will be the last. Or that this is the last person. The addiction goes on. You keep looking. Keep chasing. Keep justifying. Keep lying to yourself. Until one day, you stare into the mirror and see someone else looking back at you. It is not always dramatic. Sometimes it is just a small thing: a secret text thread, an erased browser history, a relationship slowly falling apart while you pretend it is okay. Lust never takes everything at once. Lust convinces you to surrender it bit by bit.

"The fire we think we hold in hand,
Will burn the soul we cannot stand."

14

When Love and Lust Collide

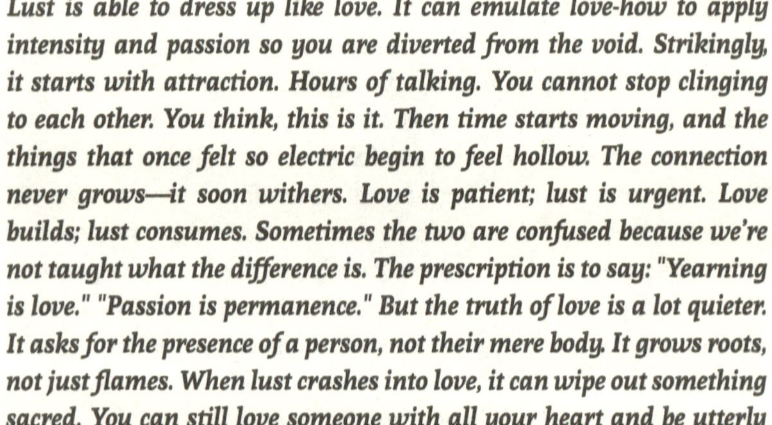

Lust is able to dress up like love. It can emulate love-how to apply intensity and passion so you are diverted from the void. Strikingly, it starts with attraction. Hours of talking. You cannot stop clinging to each other. You think, this is it. Then time starts moving, and the things that once felt so electric begin to feel hollow. The connection never grows—it soon withers. Love is patient; lust is urgent. Love builds; lust consumes. Sometimes the two are confused because we're not taught what the difference is. The prescription is to say: "Yearning is love." "Passion is permanence." But the truth of love is a lot quieter. It asks for the presence of a person, not their mere body. It grows roots, not just flames. When lust crashes into love, it can wipe out something sacred. You can still love someone with all your heart and be utterly consumed by desire for somebody else. That is the tragedy. Lust needs no reasons- it only needs opportunities. When lust wins, love usually loses.

"Lust will wear love's borrowed face,
Until it's torn in passion's place."

15

Media and Lust: The Connection

❦

The media greatly influences our ideas of lust. Regarding advertising and entertainment, the bounds for sexual themes and imagery are endless. This can have the effect of normalizing and glorifying lustful behavior by the continuous bombardment associated with it, hence making popularization of healthy attitudes toward sexuality rather challenging. Media reflects society's lust and amplifies it into an unstoppable raging river of images, stories, and symbols, all meant to captivate and provoke. In this whirling pool, lust is packaged and sold sometimes as innocent fantasy, at others as a dire need, thereby affecting the very perception of the individual on concepts of attraction, beauty, and fulfillment. Media confuses the lines between a genuine attraction and mere superficial allure, often commodifying desire instead of commodifying it as something to be felt. Yet at the same time, the opportunities it offers to challenge taboos, open up conversations, and reshape healthy, alternate expressions of passion are immense.

"Media doesn't just mirror lust—it magnifies and molds it, turning desire into a commodity while blurring the lines between true connection and surface allure, yet also holding the power to rewrite the story of passion."

16

Technology and the Perpetuation of Desire

The advent of the Internet and other digital technologies has changed the feel and expression of lust. Online platforms bring into reach the ease of access to explicit content, very often blurring boundaries between public and private spaces. This is therefore going to pose new challenges in dealing with issues of ethics and social reality on lust within the digital age. Technology changes lust from a momentary feeling to an ever-present experience to be gratified instantly via screens of all sorts. A swipe or two, a tap of the finger, or a bit of streaming: turning desire into an on-demand digital product that is hired, rushed, or sold. The algorithms learn what excites, what feeds temptation, and then repeat it-until it becomes a loop in which desire is never quite satisfied. Yet, the tech that helps empower sexual expressions and relations simultaneously isolates, converting human emotion into patterns of consumption. In this world, lust is no longer just a private feeling but rather data that can be marketed, measured, and at least spoken for data source able to echo limits by pixels and platforms, all too often sidestepping the wretched body yearning to be touched.

"In the digital age, lust no longer flickers briefly—it streams endlessly, shaped by algorithms that turn desire into data, isolating the soul behind screens while feeding an insatiable loop of craving."

17

The Broken Aftermath

No one condemns the residue. They will not show you those moments of solar glare in the kitchen after a bare truth is let the look in the eyes of someone who had trusted you; the first stirrings of self-hatred engendered inside, yet outside on the surface, you pretend as if all were fine . Sometimes, you have no manifestation out there in the aftermath of lust. It is not just about broken relationships; it is about broken spirits. It is about waking up next to a stranger who somehow uplifts you less than before. It is about shame that crawls right beneath the skin. It is regret that is already behind the car. Drug. Affair. Lie. Compulsiveness. It's not just about behaviors-they are the symptoms. Symptoms of an achromatic pain, of an unresolved hunger. After lust has eaten its fill, it never stays to clean the mess-they just leave you alone, sitting there wondering how an adulterer and a short while ago felt so good became something that hurts so bad.

"The morning finds what night conceals,
The aching cost that pleasure steals."

18

The Curse Revealed

Here it is, the truth we avoid in general: Lust, if not kept in check, is bondage; it is not freedom. It turns persons into things; it renders love into a mere transaction. It takes away the sanctity of intimacy. You stop seeing the other as a person and start seeing them as an object to satiate your hunger . And gradually, you cease to see yourself as well. The curse is not merely about what lust does to your relationships but what it does to your soul. The guilt. The numbness. The hollow victories. You gain what you want but lose what you need. You satisfy the urge, starving the heart. It keeps you wanting and never fulfilling . And the most bitter part is that it convinces you that this time will be different; that the next body, the next night, the next high will finally bring peace. But peace never resides in lust. It only lives in love. In truth.

"The more I fed, the more I bled,
The hunger grew with all I shed."

19

How to Overcome Lust for Personal Growth

———◦♡◦———

There are also some instance levers: Mindfulness practices, therapy, and the building of good habits make up a core part of establishing self-awareness, discipline, and support needed to overcome lust. In a similar vein, it is through strong, respectful relationships that an outlet to healthily manage one's desires can be found. Getting out of lust at all does not mean repression; it means conversion into a higher, conscious energy along the path of conscious transformation from pure craving to core clarity. It can start by being conscious about it: noticing how lust arises, what triggers lust, and what deeper need is covered in disguise by lust, if that is loneliness, some insecurity, boredom, or a genuine hunger for connection. Instead of chasing after this feeling or trying to get rid of it through shame, growth occurs when you meet it with curiosity and discipline and learn to return the energy into creativity, purpose, or purified love based on respect. So in this sense, lust becomes a school for the development of emotional intelligence and self-mastery, wherein desire itself does not fade away but transforms into a wiser and meaningful.

"Lust is not to be crushed or shamed, but understood and transformed—an invitation to meet desire with curiosity and discipline, turning raw craving into creative purpose and respectful love."

20

The Role of Faith and Spirituality

Faith and spiritual values constitute the way of deliverance for so many. Religious faith teaches man how to be chaste and pure by adhering to virtuous conduct, such as chastity and self-restraint. Spiritual activities like praying, meditation, and involvement in the community further cement this principle and help a person in their growth. Faith and spirituality in a way form a serene counterweight to the storm of human desire, but rather as a subtle rhythm to live by. They somehow urge us to rise above the immediacy of gratification and ask deeper questions: What is it that I want? What nourishes the soul rather than just the senses? And in moments where lust or something similar seems to throw us off balance, spirituality puts it in perspective: we are more than our impulses. Rather, it is a different way of looking at them, a way in which desires become signs pointing toward a deeper longing for relationship, meaning, or even God. Through prayer, meditation, or spiritual discipline, people find the strength to carry out the hard transformation of bringing ephemeral urges into lasting insight, choosing not what feels good but what brings peace and fosters growth.

"I am not my impulse—I am the witness, the soul seeking depth over desire. Through faith, I return to stillness. Through spirit, I rise beyond craving."

21
Searching for Redemption

Healing doesn't come easily. You have to dig beneath the desire and ask, Is it hunger for some touch? Validation? To be known, to be seen, to be loved, and not to be used or admired? The original opportunity for redemption is honesty: Admitting there is a problem. Admitting that you have used others. Admitting that you have used yourself. You are tired. And then the work begins- therapy, confession, prayer, accountability, great boundaries. For some, it's faith. For others, recovery groups. For all, it's a return journey to self-respect, dignity, and the capability to be alone without the world crashing down. You teach yourself again how to feel, to connect, to say no to destruction, and yes to healing. You cease defining yourself by lust. Then slowly, you begin to believe you are more than your appetite.

"In ashes still, a voice remains,
To call me out from binding chains."

22

Reflection on Lust as a Curse

A vice, lust, is still a powerful, complex subject. It ties into many other factors within the human experience, including theology and psychology, social values, and morals. To consider lust means to consider its complications, the problems that lust has caused, and continues to cause, within the human experience in terms of personal and social levels. If considered a curse, lust is less an act imposed from above and more a jail made within, craving worthy of destruction as it distorts clarity and erodes control. It comes along as a package wrapped in pleasure and urgency, but in the end, it leaves behind a silent emptiness, a hunger so ravenous that feeding it only worsens. As a curse, lust is not the feeling but the loss of freedom it imparts- when desire supersedes wisdom, when bodies are chased, but meaning is absent. It binds the heart to illusions, whispering that just one touch, just one image, or just one thrill stands between us and fulfillment- what an illusion- harvested blindly, lust is killing us. To see lust as a curse is to throw away shame and view it with sober eyes: as a force that lures us into the trade of depth for distraction and freedom for fixation.

"Lust is not the enemy—attachment is. When desire clouds the soul, let awareness be the flame that purifies, not burns."

23

Reclaiming Intimacy

Real intimacy bears terror. Not because of the physical: Being naked is a cakewalk. The hard part is bearing your soul. Letting someone see your shame. Your fears. Your scars. But that is where real connection resides. In those unglamorous, unfiltered, and unsexy moments when somebody is looking at you-really looking at you-and stays. To reclaim intimacy is to choose to be present rather than perform. It is about seeking emotional closeness before sexual gratification. To allow sex to serve as an expression of love rather than a replacement for it. It takes time. It takes courage. And when in someone's arms, you feel safe-not just wanted, but safe-your past is just that, a past you were settling for." And there's no way "back" anymore.

"To hold with heart, not hands alone,
Is how the soul comes safely home."

24

Moving Forward: Personal and Societal Change

⟶♡⟵

Controlling lust calls for a harmonious approach that incorporates moral guidance, psychological support, and social awareness. Societies can thereby alter or minimize the negative effects of lust on people by providing an environment in which positive regard toward sexuality and relationships is developed. Individual determination and commitment to growth and self-discipline, if united with efforts by society, no doubt would bring about change and be the key toward a understanding of lust as a sin. Desires may be reimagined in terms of how one relates to them. Individually speaking, this means taking cognizance of learning to pause rather than react swiftly, and gathering raw impulses into acts or forms of connection, creativity, or compassion. It is not the suppression of lust; rather, it is its sublimation and maturation. On a broad societal scope, change occurs when society stops objectifying desire, i.e., when the media, education, and culture stop pandering to lust as an act of conquest and begin awarding dignity to intimacy as an act of understanding. True progress happens when desire is no longer considered shameful but neither is permitted to rule us.

"True freedom is not found in denying desire, but in rising above it—where passion becomes purpose, and lust bows to love guided by wisdom."

25
A New Way to Love

Some say love is like a crazy, loud boom of fireworks lighting up the skies. I like to think of it as a garden needing consistent nurturing. All this requires patience. Nurturing. Care. You do not just fall into love—you build it. You stay when things become boring. You show up when times are tough . The new way of being with someone stands for choosing connection over chemistry. Depth over blowing off steam. It asks: How do I serve this person? Rather than: What can I get from them? Then you also have to start loving yourself. And no, not shallow, hashtag loving. But real loving: Give acceptance to your past. Forgive yourself for your mistakes. Rewrite your story from cursed to called. Called to something deeper. Truer. Holier.

> "I found in quiet, faithful grace,
> A fiercer love in a softer place."

Epilogue: Living Beyond The Curse

You are not your past. You are not your worst mistake. Not your deepest shame. Not your hunger. Lust might have been a little shaping force in your story, but it has no say in how the story ends. You are capable of being loved in a way that does not destroy you, of desiring that does not overpower you, and of living a life where the body and soul meld together, not cause a rift between them. Just the first step. Then another. And then one more. Until it is—almost—just a memory. And slowly, softly, you walk into independence.

"The curse once named me with its flame,
But now I walk with love, not shame."

Prabh Jot Singh is a celebrated, best-selling author widely recognized for his intriguing book, Psycho Imaginations. His exceptional career spans multiple professions, earning him a place as a world record holder in numerous fields, as documented in the Prestigious Book of World Records.

In addition to his literary success, Singh holds a Master's degree in Sociology and has earned over 40 diplomas and certifications from top institutions across the UK, USA, Dubai, the Netherlands, and beyond. His outstanding contributions have been honored with prestigious accolades, including the Vishwa Ratna Sammaan Award and the International Star Award, underscoring his global impact.

Singh's remarkable achievements reflect his exceptional expertise, dedication, and commitment to excellence across diverse disciplines, making him a distinguished figure in both academic and professional realms.

Connect With Author:

Stay connected and be the first to explore new works from this author by following their journey on social media!
Your honest reviews light the way for fellow readers, guiding them to uncover this book's hidden depths.
We embrace all feedback, whether it uplifts or offers thoughtful insights, as it helps us grow together.
If this book resonated with you, pass it forward and share the experience with someone special!
Use the QR code below to connect:

Step Into My World — Scan the QR Code to Reach Me!